SMARTIN-UP™ YOUR PROFESSIONALISM

In 365 TWEETS

Sindy Martin

Willway Publishing, Inc.

ISBN: 0982935706
ISBN-13: 9780982935705

PRINTED IN THE UNITED STATES OF AMERICA

This book is dedicated to my best friend

Lubna Sachedina Reece

who has believed in me since the
very day she met me.

A NOTE FROM SINDY

My passion is helping people learn new skills that will bring them happiness and success in their personal and business lives. I have done this for many years and will continue to do so until the day I leave this earth.

I have found a common thread among the people whom I have instructed, regardless of the topic. They want just the "steps" - the key information that will immediately affect them as people and in their jobs.

I post a Smartin-Up Your Professionalism Tip on Twitter Daily, so follow me at **_www.twitter.com/SindyMartin_** to learn new skills, tricks and receive gentle reminders that will have an immediate impact on your life and help you "Smartin-Up™" your personal brand and your professional presence.

I wish you great happiness and success in life!

Sincerely,

Sindy

SMARTIN-UP™ YOUR PROFESSIONALISM

Professionals know that the control center of your life is your attitude.

SMARTIN-UP™ YOUR PROFESSIONALISM

Are you a good participant in your social media relationship? Relationships always require the participation of both parties.

SMARTIN-UP™ YOUR PROFESSIONALISM

Are your eyeglasses up to date or do they date you...

SMARTIN-UP™ YOUR PROFESSIONALISM

Ask permission before entering a co-workers cubicle.

SMARTIN-UP™ YOUR PROFESSIONALISM

At the table, your drink is on the right and your bread plate is on the left.

SMARTIN-UP™ YOUR PROFESSIONALISM

Backing your car into a parking space can be perceived as being ready to leave before you even arrived.

SMARTIN-UP™ YOUR PROFESSIONALISM

Be careful that your body language matches your words. 55% Body Language, 38% Tone of Voice, 7% Words.

SMARTIN-UP™ YOUR PROFESSIONALISM

Be polite by not monopolizing someone's time at a networking event. Most people have a goal to meet 5 to 8 people at an event.

SMARTIN-UP™ YOUR PROFESSIONALISM

Be sure that you have the person's attention before you start speaking.

SMARTIN-UP™ YOUR PROFESSIONALISM

Be the first to speak. Walk up and introduce yourself.

SMARTIN-UP™ YOUR PROFESSIONALISM

Being confident that your manners are up to date makes for a more enjoyable dinner, meeting, networking...

SMARTIN-UP™ YOUR PROFESSIONALISM

Business casual is no longer very casual. Step it up tomorrow and look polished. They will notice.

SMARTIN-UP™ YOUR PROFESSIONALISM

Chewing gum is the same as chewing a big piece of food. Not attractive!

SMARTIN-UP™ YOUR PROFESSIONALISM

Develop good telephone skills: Speak clearly, be courteous, leave concise messages & return calls promptly.

SMARTIN-UP™ YOUR PROFESSIONALISM

When eating, do not hold your fork or spoon as if it were a shovel.

SMARTIN-UP™ YOUR PROFESSIONALISM

Do you lead or do you manage? People follow leaders. Help others develop to their true potential.

SMARTIN-UP™ YOUR PROFESSIONALISM

Do you/your employees dress too casual? Being too casual can lead to casualties!

SMARTIN-UP™ YOUR PROFESSIONALISM

Don't Be Rude/Gross - If you have a sinus infection/cold, try not to audibly clear the mucus from the nasal passage to the throat.

SMARTIN-UP™ YOUR PROFESSIONALISM

Refrain from recording, long, cutesy voice mail messages or greetings that sound unprofessional.

SMARTIN-UP™ YOUR PROFESSIONALISM

Even though the weather is bad, it is important to keep our cars clean both inside and out.

SMARTIN-UP™ YOUR PROFESSIONALISM

Excitement is contagious. Develop a natural excitement about meeting your goals today.

SMARTIN-UP™ YOUR PROFESSIONALISM

For the sanity of your host/hostess, don't arrive early to a party.

SMARTIN-UP™ YOUR PROFESSIONALISM

Have a daily plan. Without a plan, the day can be lost before it starts.

SMARTIN-UP™ YOUR PROFESSIONALISM

Hold yourself responsible for a higher standard than anybody expects of you.

SMARTIN-UP™ YOUR PROFESSIONALISM

How we dress directly affects our job performance.

SMARTIN-UP™ YOUR PROFESSIONALISM

If asked where you want to eat, give 3 suggestions of moderately priced restaurants that you like.

SMARTIN-UP™ YOUR PROFESSIONALISM

If someone drops something or is struggling to carry something, immediately ask if you can help.

SMARTIN-UP™ YOUR PROFESSIONALISM

If you are going to be speaking in front of a group of people, dress professionally.

SMARTIN-UP™ YOUR PROFESSIONALISM

If you have called a number by accident don't just hang up. Simply say "Excuse me, I've dialed the wrong number."

SMARTIN-UP™ YOUR PROFESSIONALISM

If you reach a door first, man or woman, you should open it, go through it and then hold it open for others.

SMARTIN-UP™ YOUR PROFESSIONALISM

If you want to succeed, run with the "Thoroughbreds." They are netweavers.

SMARTIN-UP™ YOUR PROFESSIONALISM

Ignoring conflict will not "make it go away." Practice conflict resolution so you get good at it.

SMARTIN-UP™ YOUR PROFESSIONALISM

It doesn't sound very professional to say "and all that stuff" or "stuff like that." Be clear and precise.

SMARTIN-UP™ YOUR PROFESSIONALISM

It is not proper to tuck your tie into your shirt, or throw it over your shoulder, while eating.

SMARTIN-UP™ YOUR PROFESSIONALISM

It's important to chew with your mouth closed, especially while eating buffalo wings!

SMARTIN-UP™ YOUR PROFESSIONALISM

Keep breath mints in your car in a visible place. Bad breath ruins business!

SMARTIN-UP™ YOUR PROFESSIONALISM

Learn to keep a pleasant look on your face, but save that BIG smile for when you shake someone's hand.

SMARTIN-UP™ YOUR PROFESSIONALISM

Look people in the eye and smile. Be kind to your fellow human beings.

SMARTIN-UP™ YOUR PROFESSIONALISM

Many people have helped you this week, call/send a quick "thank you" to let them know you appreciate them.

SMARTIN-UP™ YOUR PROFESSIONALISM

No one is infallible. Call attention to people's mistakes indirectly. Share knowledge and kindness.

SMARTIN-UP™ YOUR PROFESSIONALISM

On Twitter, if people follow you, it's polite to "follow" them back.

SMARTIN-UP™ YOUR PROFESSIONALISM

Paradigm Shift: 1st Call, 2nd Email, 3rd Text. Only through a phone call can I hear your tone of voice.

SMARTIN-UP™ YOUR PROFESSIONALISM

Please do not talk to another store associate while waiting on a customer.

SMARTIN-UP™ YOUR PROFESSIONALISM

Please refrain from digging the wax out of your ear in public.

SMARTIN-UP™ YOUR PROFESSIONALISM

Professionals & Parents delegate. They know it is how we help our team/employees/ children grow. Let them do it their way.

SMARTIN-UP™ YOUR PROFESSIONALISM

Professionals exercise their brain and vocabulary on a daily basis.

SMARTIN-UP™ YOUR PROFESSIONALISM

Professionals keep their bad days to themselves and leave negative attitudes at home. Focus on the positive!

SMARTIN-UP™ YOUR PROFESSIONALISM

A transformational leader has a vision and a deep passion which inspires others to achieve great things.

SMARTIN-UP™ YOUR PROFESSIONALISM

Professionals set goals for the week and keep those goals in front of them. Read them daily, make them happen!

SMARTIN-UP™ YOUR PROFESSIONALISM

Putting role models on pedestals only further separates you from them. We all have strengths and weaknesses.

SMARTIN-UP™ YOUR PROFESSIONALISM

Refrain from being in front of your email on the pc or smartphone when talking on the phone. Pay attention to the caller.

SMARTIN-UP™ YOUR PROFESSIONALISM

Refrain from using a toothpick in public and please don't walk around with one hanging out of your mouth.

SMARTIN-UP™ YOUR PROFESSIONALISM

Remember to keep one hand in your lap while eating. Two handed eating is poor form.

SMARTIN-UP™ YOUR PROFESSIONALISM

Remember to wear your name tag on the right side of your jacket.

SMARTIN-UP™ YOUR PROFESSIONALISM

Seeking advice is a sign of strength, not a sign of weakness. Choose a mentor with values similar to yours.

SMARTIN-UP™ YOUR PROFESSIONALISM

Showing respect for another's cultural practices will often result in reciprocal respect being shown to yours.

SMARTIN-UP™ YOUR PROFESSIONALISM

Start your meeting at exactly the time you planned for it to start. Respect those who arrived on time.

SMARTIN-UP™ YOUR PROFESSIONALISM

Take a look at your briefcase/computer bag/satchel. What does it say about you...frayed, dirty, dusty...

SMARTIN-UP™ YOUR PROFESSIONALISM

Take time to understand the generational differences. It will enhance your communication skills.

SMARTIN-UP™ YOUR PROFESSIONALISM

The only proper place to chew gum is in private, never in public. Very distracting and sometimes disgusting.

SMARTIN-UP™ YOUR PROFESSIONALISM

Think of your surroundings and other people when choosing the umbrella you will wield on a rainy day.

SMARTIN-UP™ YOUR PROFESSIONALISM

Try not to clink the side of your glass while stirring your coffee or tea.

SMARTIN-UP™ YOUR PROFESSIONALISM

Try to evaluate problems, not symptoms. Look for what causes the symptom. Believe in people.

SMARTIN-UP™ YOUR PROFESSIONALISM

Using good manners shows you have confidence, self-esteem and success. How are your manners?

SMARTIN-UP™ YOUR PROFESSIONALISM

We all have our favorite shirts, but once they begin to look worn we need to get rid of them.

SMARTIN-UP™ YOUR PROFESSIONALISM

Wearing more than one ring on each hand is not considered very professional.

SMARTIN-UP™ YOUR PROFESSIONALISM

When an invitation has an RSVP it is proper to respond as quickly as possible.

SMARTIN-UP™ YOUR PROFESSIONALISM

When disinterested in a conversation, but need to be polite, look interested by counting their blinks.

SMARTIN-UP™ YOUR PROFESSIONALISM

When in conversations, professionals listen 80% of the time and talk 20% of the time.

SMARTIN-UP™ YOUR PROFESSIONALISM

When leaving voice mail messages, be very brief and speak slowly. State your number at the beginning and end.

SMARTIN-UP™ YOUR PROFESSIONALISM

When networking, develop a great moving on strategy so you do not spend too much time in one place.

SMARTIN-UP™ YOUR PROFESSIONALISM

When someone gives you a compliment, thank them sincerely.

SMARTIN-UP™ YOUR PROFESSIONALISM

When was the last time you cleaned and polished your shoes?

SMARTIN-UP™ YOUR PROFESSIONALISM

When was the last time you sent someone a handwritten thank you note?

SMARTIN-UP™ YOUR PROFESSIONALISM

When you avoid gossip and complaining you are seen as more professional and trustworthy.

SMARTIN-UP™ YOUR PROFESSIONALISM

When you have to cancel an appointment, it is better to do it by phone than email.

SMARTIN-UP™ YOUR PROFESSIONALISM

While driving If you can hear/see an emergency vehicle with lights on, pull to the side of the road as quickly and safely as possible.

SMARTIN-UP™ YOUR PROFESSIONALISM

Wisdom comes in silence. Take time this weekend to quietly sit and reflect.

SMARTIN-UP™ YOUR PROFESSIONALISM

YES, it is rude to wear your bluetooth earpiece while sitting in a meeting!

SMARTIN-UP™ YOUR PROFESSIONALISM

You may have all the sales training and negotiating skills, but unless you have manners they will not buy!

SMARTIN-UP™ YOUR PROFESSIONALISM

Your career and your company's future can be advanced or jeopardized at business dining events.

SMARTIN-UP™ YOUR PROFESSIONALISM

When someone scratches the tip of their nose or their neck while answering a question, they could be lying.

SMARTIN-UP™ YOUR PROFESSIONALISM

Professionals practice forgiveness because they know it is the way to mentor and set examples for others.

SMARTIN-UP™ YOUR PROFESSIONALISM

Do not ask if you can bring your pet to someone's home. The host will let you know if your pet is welcome.

SMARTIN-UP™ YOUR PROFESSIONALISM

A leader respects others for their talents and abilities. They take every opportunity to tell them.

SMARTIN-UP™ YOUR PROFESSIONALISM

After finishing your meal, do not push your plate away. Leave it in place for the wait staff to take away.

SMARTIN-UP™ YOUR PROFESSIONALISM

Are you dressing too casual at the office? Get spiffy! If you look professional, and act professional, you will get noticed.

SMARTIN-UP™ YOUR PROFESSIONALISM

Arriving 5 to 10 minutes ahead of time for a meeting shows respect for the organizer's time.

SMARTIN-UP™ YOUR PROFESSIONALISM

Ask someone how they are doing today, then actually listen to the answer. Make someone's day!

SMARTIN-UP™ YOUR PROFESSIONALISM

Avoid "cell yell." Remember to use your regular conversational tone when speaking on your cell phone.

SMARTIN-UP™ YOUR PROFESSIONALISM

Be aware of other people around you. Try not to step in front of someone in an aisle. Say excuse me.

SMARTIN-UP™ YOUR PROFESSIONALISM

Be careful with your corporate gift giving in the office. It is easy to offend others unintentionally.

SMARTIN-UP™ YOUR PROFESSIONALISM

Be polite by not starting to eat until everyone at the table has been served.

SMARTIN-UP™ YOUR PROFESSIONALISM

Be sure to clean your eyeglasses on a daily basis. Dirty eyeglasses are very distracting and unprofessional.

SMARTIN-UP™ YOUR PROFESSIONALISM

Be the one that lets others go first, that lets that car come into your lane, and the one that says hello.

SMARTIN-UP™ YOUR PROFESSIONALISM

Build quality relationships. A person willing to go the extra mile to help you is worth more than 10 people who will not.

SMARTIN-UP™ YOUR PROFESSIONALISM

Butter is placed on a baked potato with a fork, not with a knife.

SMARTIN-UP™ YOUR PROFESSIONALISM

Compliment at least 3 people today for something they did, what they said, their attitude.....

SMARTIN-UP™ YOUR PROFESSIONALISM

Did you know that there is a proper way to eat each type of fruit?

SMARTIN-UP™ YOUR PROFESSIONALISM

When sharing a story, try to keep the length of the story to 4 minutes.

SMARTIN-UP™ YOUR PROFESSIONALISM

Do you make positive visual impressions? Dress for success!

SMARTIN-UP™ YOUR PROFESSIONALISM

Don't ask the host of a party for a tour of their house unless it's a housewarming.

SMARTIN-UP™ YOUR PROFESSIONALISM

Don't bring a guest to an event unless you have gotten permission from the host or hostess.

SMARTIN-UP™ YOUR PROFESSIONALISM

Don't share someone's good news (or bad news) without asking them first!

SMARTIN-UP™ YOUR PROFESSIONALISM

Whenever you are with someone, especially a child, and you observe someone being considerate to another, point it out.

SMARTIN-UP™ YOUR PROFESSIONALISM

Five frequently misspelled words: calendar, cemetery, conscience, conscious and conscientious.

SMARTIN-UP™ YOUR PROFESSIONALISM

Forget the "hat hair", take your hat off when you are inside a business or restaurant. It's polite!

SMARTIN-UP™ YOUR PROFESSIONALISM

Have you set your attitude goal for this year? Mine's "Where there is a will, there is a way." What's yours?

SMARTIN-UP™ YOUR PROFESSIONALISM

How (and if) we greet others says a lot about who we are and our integrity. Do you speak first?

SMARTIN-UP™ YOUR PROFESSIONALISM

How's your time management? What small tasks are taking your time that could be done by others? Delegate!

SMARTIN-UP™ YOUR PROFESSIONALISM

If both forks are the same size, which do you use for your salad? Use the fork to the farthest left.

SMARTIN-UP™ YOUR PROFESSIONALISM

If someone has called and left a message on your cell phone, it is rude to just text them back.

SMARTIN-UP™ YOUR PROFESSIONALISM

If you back your car into a parking space it gives the impression that you can't wait to leave.

SMARTIN-UP™ YOUR PROFESSIONALISM

If you have something trapped between your teeth, don't pick at it while you are at the table.

SMARTIN-UP™ YOUR PROFESSIONALISM

If you really want something you have to give it your all and then go a step further.

SMARTIN-UP™ YOUR PROFESSIONALISM

If you want your email message to be read, keep it short, to the point and have a relevant subject!

SMARTIN-UP™ YOUR PROFESSIONALISM

In American business situations, both men and women should stand when being introduced.

SMARTIN-UP™ YOUR PROFESSIONALISM

It is best not to place your briefcase or purse on the conference room table during a meeting.

SMARTIN-UP™ YOUR PROFESSIONALISM

It is rude to finish the other person's thought or sentence. Refrain from interrupting.

SMARTIN-UP™ YOUR PROFESSIONALISM

It is very rude to spit in public.

SMARTIN-UP™ YOUR PROFESSIONALISM

Keep emails brief and to the point. Always have a greeting and a closing.

SMARTIN-UP™ YOUR PROFESSIONALISM

Try not to criticize, condemn or complain at work or at the office.

SMARTIN-UP™ YOUR PROFESSIONALISM

Looking professional includes wearing up-to-date eyeglasses, both regular and reading glasses.

SMARTIN-UP™ YOUR PROFESSIONALISM

Many people read lips when networking in loud venues. Keep your face in view and enunciate your words.

SMARTIN-UP™ YOUR PROFESSIONALISM

Nose rings, lip and tongue piercing, and any other body hardware should be invisible at work.

SMARTIN-UP™ YOUR PROFESSIONALISM

Once a week have lunch with someone in another department or industry. Broaden your knowledge base.

SMARTIN-UP™ YOUR PROFESSIONALISM

People cannot hear you nod your head in approval/disapproval over the phone, you must verbalize feelings.

SMARTIN-UP™ YOUR PROFESSIONALISM

Please do not email your dentist/doctor the night before your appt to cancel. Call them!

SMARTIN-UP™ YOUR PROFESSIONALISM

Please refrain from answering your cell phone in a public restroom.

SMARTIN-UP™ YOUR PROFESSIONALISM

Professionals and Parents know that they are always being observed and must conduct themselves accordingly.

SMARTIN-UP™ YOUR PROFESSIONALISM

Professionals exercise their mind, body and soul on a daily basis. The 3 keys to a happy, healthy you!

SMARTIN-UP™ YOUR PROFESSIONALISM

Professionals know that communication can always be improved. They take courses to improve their skills.

SMARTIN-UP™ YOUR PROFESSIONALISM

Professionals know the difference between appropriate and inappropriate displays of anger.

SMARTIN-UP™ YOUR PROFESSIONALISM

Professionals spend more time reading than watching television and encourage others to do the same.

SMARTIN-UP™ YOUR PROFESSIONALISM

Q: What is an example of the worst bad manners? A: To hurt someone's feelings.

SMARTIN-UP™ YOUR PROFESSIONALISM

Always keep mints with you. A mint is the preferred way to freshen your breath, not chewing gum or candy.

SMARTIN-UP™ YOUR PROFESSIONALISM

Remember that the words "hell" and "damn" are profanity. Professionals do not use profanity.

SMARTIN-UP™ YOUR PROFESSIONALISM

Remember to keep your elbows close to your body while cutting the food on your plate.

SMARTIN-UP™ YOUR PROFESSIONALISM

Remembering to use our basic manners applies at home as well as when we are in public.

SMARTIN-UP™ YOUR PROFESSIONALISM

Try to make appointments with someone over the phone. Asking them to look at your calendar on-line can be perceived as arrogant.

SMARTIN-UP™ YOUR PROFESSIONALISM

Make sure your clothing is spot free; food on your clothes speaks volumes.

SMARTIN-UP™ YOUR PROFESSIONALISM

Studies show that people that talk too fast tend to be insecure and suffer from low self-esteem.

SMARTIN-UP™ YOUR PROFESSIONALISM

Take action to develop a more positive attitude.

SMARTIN-UP™ YOUR PROFESSIONALISM

Talking too fast or talking too slow have the same effect on people. And it is not good.

SMARTIN-UP™ YOUR PROFESSIONALISM

The quality of your writing matters online because it is all we see of you. So spelling and grammar do count!

SMARTIN-UP™ YOUR PROFESSIONALISM

Tired of poor customer service? Politely say something.

SMARTIN-UP™ YOUR PROFESSIONALISM

Try not to over think a thank you note so much that you don't even send one. Keep it simple and heart felt.

SMARTIN-UP™ YOUR PROFESSIONALISM

Try to refrain from interrupting a person who is talking. If you do before they are finished, apologize.

SMARTIN-UP™ YOUR PROFESSIONALISM

Using your cell phone to check the time can be perceived as rude. Better to wear a watch and glance at it.

SMARTIN-UP™ YOUR PROFESSIONALISM

We form impressions visually (55%), vocally (your voice 38%) and verbally (what you say 7%) in 4-7 seconds.

SMARTIN-UP™ YOUR PROFESSIONALISM

What action did you take today to get one step closer to your goal?

SMARTIN-UP™ YOUR PROFESSIONALISM

When asked to pass the salt, always pass the salt and pepper together. It shows you have manners!

SMARTIN-UP™ YOUR PROFESSIONALISM

When eating, men should not tuck their tie into their shirt or put their tie over their shoulder.

SMARTIN-UP™ YOUR PROFESSIONALISM

When introduced to a veteran or someone serving in the military, thank them. They protect your rights and your country.

SMARTIN-UP™ YOUR PROFESSIONALISM

When lost in thought, be sure that you keep your lips together. A mouth hanging open is not flattering.

SMARTIN-UP™ YOUR PROFESSIONALISM

When replying to an email, give a point of reference, not just the answer, and include your signature line.

SMARTIN-UP™ YOUR PROFESSIONALISM

When someone scratches the tip of their nose or their neck while answering a question, they could be lying.

SMARTIN-UP™ YOUR PROFESSIONALISM

When was the last time you cleaned your watch and jewelry? Use jewelry cleaner and polishing cloths weekly.

SMARTIN-UP™ YOUR PROFESSIONALISM

When writing an email, keep it brief and to the point. One huge paragraph may not be read at all.

SMARTIN-UP™ YOUR PROFESSIONALISM

When you call someone, be sure to ask "Have I caught you at a good time to talk?" Respect their time.

SMARTIN-UP™ YOUR PROFESSIONALISM

When you present your business card to someone, hold the corner of the card and make sure it is facing them.

SMARTIN-UP™ YOUR PROFESSIONALISM

While in the airport, remember that there is always someone behind you. Try not to stop suddenly.

SMARTIN-UP™ YOUR PROFESSIONALISM

Women in business should refrain from nodding in agreement unless they truly agree with what is being said.

SMARTIN-UP™ YOUR PROFESSIONALISM

Yes, there is a correct way to walk up and down the stairs.

SMARTIN-UP™ YOUR PROFESSIONALISM

You may think you can avoid communicating by being silent. But your silence speaks.

SMARTIN-UP™ YOUR PROFESSIONALISM

Your commitment must be stronger than your obstacles.

SMARTIN-UP™ YOUR PROFESSIONALISM

Remember to polish/clean your shoes, belt, computer bag and/or purse on a regular basis. Look polished!

SMARTIN-UP™ YOUR PROFESSIONALISM

Professionals refrain from you using absolutes (like always or never) because they can lead to arguments.

SMARTIN-UP™ YOUR PROFESSIONALISM

Please be polite and park your car between the two white lines designated for one parking space.

SMARTIN-UP™ YOUR PROFESSIONALISM

A participative leader allows others to participate in the decision making process, then makes the decision.

SMARTIN-UP™ YOUR PROFESSIONALISM

After sitting down at the table and waiting for everyone else to sit down, unfold your napkin and place it in your lap.

SMARTIN-UP™ YOUR PROFESSIONALISM

Always listen when someone is speaking to you. You never know where that jewel of advice will come from.

SMARTIN-UP™ YOUR PROFESSIONALISM

Are you getting too casual with those close to you? Please and Thank You are still the magic words!

SMARTIN-UP™ YOUR PROFESSIONALISM

As men age hair begins to grow on their ears. Have your barber or significant other trim them for you.

SMARTIN-UP™ YOUR PROFESSIONALISM

Ask the host/hostess of an event who they think you should meet. They will be glad to introduce you.

SMARTIN-UP™ YOUR PROFESSIONALISM

Avoid side conversations and interruptions while on the phone. Ask permission to leave the call for a moment.

SMARTIN-UP™ YOUR PROFESSIONALISM

Be aware of people walking behind you where ever you are. Try not to stop abruptly or walk too slowly.

SMARTIN-UP™ YOUR PROFESSIONALISM

Be friendly and talk with everyone, not just a few people. Step out of your comfort zone and mingle!

SMARTIN-UP™ YOUR PROFESSIONALISM

Be polite, avoid answering a call while you are still engaged in conversation with someone else.

SMARTIN-UP™ YOUR PROFESSIONALISM

Be sure to match the mood of the person you are having a conversation with, perky and serious don't mix!

SMARTIN-UP™ YOUR PROFESSIONALISM

Be very careful with your words, they will be repeated and you won't be there to explain what you meant.

SMARTIN-UP™ YOUR PROFESSIONALISM

Business cards should never be exchanged while we are eating.

SMARTIN-UP™ YOUR PROFESSIONALISM

Call one of your customers this morning and tell them how much you appreciate their business. Do it now!

SMARTIN-UP™ YOUR PROFESSIONALISM

Consider this paradigm shift – Meet in Person, Call on Phone, Send Email, Send Text Message, Tweet.

SMARTIN-UP™ YOUR PROFESSIONALISM

Do not answer the phone while you are eating or chewing gum.

SMARTIN-UP™ YOUR PROFESSIONALISM

It is better to try to start a conversation with someone at the dessert table rather than in line at the bar.

SMARTIN-UP™ YOUR PROFESSIONALISM

Do you swim in the big tank or are you limiting yourself in the small tank?

SMARTIN-UP™ YOUR PROFESSIONALISM

Don't ask for food or a drink at a meeting unless refreshments are being offered.

SMARTIN-UP™ YOUR PROFESSIONALISM

You should not clean up spills with your own napkin and don't touch items that have dropped on the floor. Simply and politely ask your server for assistance.

SMARTIN-UP™ YOUR PROFESSIONALISM

It is not polite to wipe your plate with your bread.

SMARTIN-UP™ YOUR PROFESSIONALISM

Ever seen someone with their mouth just hanging open? Not an attractive (or professional) sight!

SMARTIN-UP™ YOUR PROFESSIONALISM

Fashion or just good professionalism? It is not acceptable in most situations for men to wear sandals with business suits.

SMARTIN-UP™ YOUR PROFESSIONALISM

Gentlemen be sure to clean your ties. Dust, bacteria and viruses attach to clothing, that includes ties.

SMARTIN-UP™ YOUR PROFESSIONALISM

Having a loud tone associated with your incoming text messages can be very annoying to those around you.

SMARTIN-UP™ YOUR PROFESSIONALISM

How civil are you? Do you greet people with a simple "Hello" whether you know them or not?

SMARTIN-UP™ YOUR PROFESSIONALISM

If a CEO asked you to come to his office right now, what impression would your appearance today make?

SMARTIN-UP™ YOUR PROFESSIONALISM

If every product you put on in the morning has a different scent, you may have a strong aroma.......

SMARTIN-UP™ YOUR PROFESSIONALISM

Become a powerful resource for others. This keeps you visible to them. Give and you shall receive!

SMARTIN-UP™ YOUR PROFESSIONALISM

If you cannot button your jacket, or it pulls the fabric too tight when you button it, do not wear it.

SMARTIN-UP™ YOUR PROFESSIONALISM

If you inadvertently hurt someone's feelings apologize immediately.

SMARTIN-UP™ YOUR PROFESSIONALISM

If you tell someone that you will call or email them, do it! Follow through with your promises.

SMARTIN-UP™ YOUR PROFESSIONALISM

If you wear sandals, be sure to keep your toe nails clean, clipped and filed.

SMARTIN-UP™ YOUR PROFESSIONALISM

In communicating with someone, what they hear is more important than what you say. Ask them what they heard.

SMARTIN-UP™ YOUR PROFESSIONALISM

It is best not to use endearments such as "Honey," "Sweetheart," or "Dear" in a business setting.

SMARTIN-UP™ YOUR PROFESSIONALISM

It is not considered professional for a woman to wear a suit or dress with bare legs. Wear hose, regardless of the weather.

SMARTIN-UP™ YOUR PROFESSIONALISM

Ladies, no nail polish is better than chipped polish. Men, get a professional to cut those cuticles.

SMARTIN-UP™ YOUR PROFESSIONALISM

Look at your fingernails and cuticles. Are you perceived as paying attention to detail?

SMARTIN-UP™ YOUR PROFESSIONALISM

Loud obnoxious laughter is rude.

SMARTIN-UP™ YOUR PROFESSIONALISM

Men and women are equal in American business. Men don't have to let a woman off the elevator before them.

SMARTIN-UP™ YOUR PROFESSIONALISM

Not wearing a wrist watch gives the impression that you do not value someone's time. Your phone is not a watch.

SMARTIN-UP™ YOUR PROFESSIONALISM

Once a word has left your mouth, there is no "undo." That impact will remain with the receiver a long time.

SMARTIN-UP™ YOUR PROFESSIONALISM

People notice the jewelry you wear. Keep it clean and polished, including your watch.

SMARTIN-UP™ YOUR PROFESSIONALISM

Please don't use cell phones or text during mealtimes.

SMARTIN-UP™ YOUR PROFESSIONALISM

Present your business card so that it can be read by the person as you hand it to them.

SMARTIN-UP™ YOUR PROFESSIONALISM

Professionals are quick to thank and show appreciation to their fellow man. They know the importance.

SMARTIN-UP™ YOUR PROFESSIONALISM

Professionals exercise their mind, soul and body daily.

SMARTIN-UP™ YOUR PROFESSIONALISM

Professionals know that in order to get optimum results they must assemble a diverse team of individuals.

SMARTIN-UP™ YOUR PROFESSIONALISM

Professionals listen more than talk. They ask questions to show that they were listening.

SMARTIN-UP™ YOUR PROFESSIONALISM

Professionals understand the importance of work/life balance. Spend time with your family!

SMARTIN-UP™ YOUR PROFESSIONALISM

Real procrastination could be a deep-seated issue such as fear of failure, fear of success or a need to control. Assess yourself.

SMARTIN-UP™ YOUR PROFESSIONALISM

Refrain from giving out someone's cell phone number or email address without his/her permission.

SMARTIN-UP™ YOUR PROFESSIONALISM

Remember to "ask" someone to do something for you, not "tell" them what to do. This applies at work and at home with our family.

SMARTIN-UP™ YOUR PROFESSIONALISM

Remember to never say things online that you wouldn't say to a person's face.

SMARTIN-UP™ YOUR PROFESSIONALISM

Reply to business emails within 24 hours, even if you don't have all the essential information.

SMARTIN-UP™ YOUR PROFESSIONALISM

Set a goal to not criticize, condemn or complain. Be positive and associate with positive people!

SMARTIN-UP™ YOUR PROFESSIONALISM

Smile! People need more smiles on Monday than any other day of the week!

SMARTIN-UP™ YOUR PROFESSIONALISM

Successful companies begin to challenge status quo and return to a real business dress code.

SMARTIN-UP™ YOUR PROFESSIONALISM

Take the initiative to make other people feel comfortable.

SMARTIN-UP™ YOUR PROFESSIONALISM

The bigger the ego the bigger the insecurities. Leaders are self-aware, self-confident and self-controlled.

SMARTIN-UP™ YOUR PROFESSIONALISM

The way we dress and groom ourselves makes an impression. Make sure it is the right impression.

SMARTIN-UP™ YOUR PROFESSIONALISM

The last Friday of the month take time to do a self-evaluation of how you did for that month. Set goals for the next month.

SMARTIN-UP™ YOUR PROFESSIONALISM

Try not to put the blame on someone else (right or wrong). It just reflects poorly on you.

SMARTIN-UP™ YOUR PROFESSIONALISM

Try to speak at a normal rate of speed, too fast or too slow, both make a poor impression.

SMARTIN-UP™ YOUR PROFESSIONALISM

Want to improve your sales......SMARTIN-UP™ your manners!
Manners matter, it's that simple!

SMARTIN-UP™ YOUR PROFESSIONALISM

We must all remember to use manners around our friends and family. It's easy to forget.

SMARTIN-UP™ YOUR PROFESSIONALISM

What course have you taken lately to refresh your leadership and management skills?

SMARTIN-UP™ YOUR PROFESSIONALISM

When attempting to solve a problem, summarize to make sure everyone has the same understanding of the situation.

SMARTIN-UP™ YOUR PROFESSIONALISM

When ever you leave a person or a group of people, say "Excuse me."

SMARTIN-UP™ YOUR PROFESSIONALISM

When introduced to someone in a wheel chair get eye level before you shake their hand. Be polite.

SMARTIN-UP™ YOUR PROFESSIONALISM

When meeting someone new, refrain from talking about ex-employers and ex-spouses. Stay in today.

SMARTIN-UP™ YOUR PROFESSIONALISM

When sending a package to a client or customer, remember to include a personal note.

SMARTIN-UP™ YOUR PROFESSIONALISM

When starting a dinner meeting or toast, never clink your glass with a utensil. Have a small bell to ring.

SMARTIN-UP™ YOUR PROFESSIONALISM

When was the last time you did something special for a member of your family?

SMARTIN-UP™ YOUR PROFESSIONALISM

When you answer the phone, please say your name. It's the polite thing to do.

SMARTIN-UP™ YOUR PROFESSIONALISM

When you encounter someone with a physical challenge, do not assume that they want your help. Ask them.

SMARTIN-UP™ YOUR PROFESSIONALISM

When you see a person that serves in your country's military say thank you or place your hand over your heart.

SMARTIN-UP™ YOUR PROFESSIONALISM

Take time to connect with a family member or friend that you have not contacted in a while.

SMARTIN-UP™ YOUR PROFESSIONALISM

Wool coats/clothing absorb cigarette smoke. Be sure to dry clean them on a regular basis.

SMARTIN-UP™ YOUR PROFESSIONALISM

You can shake hands with gloves on when you are outside, but remove your gloves before shaking hands inside.

SMARTIN-UP™ YOUR PROFESSIONALISM

You should not butter the whole piece of bread at once. This is the most common mistake made by people at a restaurant!

SMARTIN-UP™ YOUR PROFESSIONALISM

Your judgment is doubted by colleagues and superiors when you fail to use common courtesies.

SMARTIN-UP™ YOUR PROFESSIONALISM

Professionals set goals for the week and keep those goals in front of them. Read them daily, make them happen!

SMARTIN-UP™ YOUR PROFESSIONALISM

Remember to eat at the same rate as the others at the table. Try not to eat too fast or too slow.

SMARTIN-UP™ YOUR PROFESSIONALISM

A professional never passes by another human being without acknowledging them! Always say hello!

SMARTIN-UP™ YOUR PROFESSIONALISM

Allowing someone to stand around without introducing him/her can make everyone present feel uncomfortable.

SMARTIN-UP™ YOUR PROFESSIONALISM

Are you guilty of doing the "cell yell"? Do you broadcast your cell conversation in public as if your caller can't hear?

SMARTIN-UP™ YOUR PROFESSIONALISM

As the dinner host, always stand when someone new joins the table and wait until they are seated.

SMARTIN-UP™ YOUR PROFESSIONALISM

At a business dinner, don't jump right in to talking about business. Socialize first.

SMARTIN-UP™ YOUR PROFESSIONALISM

Avoid wearing big rings on your right hand so that you will not have to worry about them when you shake hands.

SMARTIN-UP™ YOUR PROFESSIONALISM

Be aware of your voice volume and adapt it to your surroundings.

SMARTIN-UP™ YOUR PROFESSIONALISM

Be friendly, people generally hope that a new acquaintance will be somebody they like.

SMARTIN-UP™ YOUR PROFESSIONALISM

Be polite, RSVP whether you can or cannot attend the event.

SMARTIN-UP™ YOUR PROFESSIONALISM

Be sure to speak to your family members as kindly as you would to a person you do business with.

SMARTIN-UP™ YOUR PROFESSIONALISM

Before forwarding an email, get permission from the sender.

SMARTIN-UP™ YOUR PROFESSIONALISM

If your hours of work are 8:00 a.m. to 5:00 p.m., that means you arrive at 7:50 a.m. and are ready to begin working at 8:00 a.m.

SMARTIN-UP™ YOUR PROFESSIONALISM

Challenge the status quo, dress business professional. People will see that you exude success.

SMARTIN-UP™ YOUR PROFESSIONALISM

Create a richer, fuller vocabulary by using a thesaurus to look up common words. Enhance your descriptions.

SMARTIN-UP™ YOUR PROFESSIONALISM

Remember not put away a person's business card until you are finished speaking with them.

SMARTIN-UP™ YOUR PROFESSIONALISM

Do you know how to shake hands properly? Are you sure? Ask someone what they think...

SMARTIN-UP™ YOUR PROFESSIONALISM

Do you talk to your employees from behind your desk or do you invite them to sit at a table beside you?

SMARTIN-UP™ YOUR PROFESSIONALISM

Refrain from asking someone else to lie for you. Having someone lie for you marks you as dishonest.

SMARTIN-UP™ YOUR PROFESSIONALISM

Please do not criticize others in public. The criticizer comes off looking worse than the person being criticized.

SMARTIN-UP™ YOUR PROFESSIONALISM

Eat at the table with your children/spouse/ significant other. We learn by example how to eat and converse properly.

SMARTIN-UP™ YOUR PROFESSIONALISM

Exaggerated praise can be taken as insincere. Use a tone of voice that shows your sincerity and honesty.

SMARTIN-UP™ YOUR PROFESSIONALISM

Fashion or just good professionalism? It is not acceptable for men to wear sandals with business suits.

SMARTIN-UP™ YOUR PROFESSIONALISM

Go through your clothes and donate all the items that look really worn.

SMARTIN-UP™ YOUR PROFESSIONALISM

Help bring back civility in the workplace. Greet and smile at EVERY person you encounter during the day.

SMARTIN-UP™ YOUR PROFESSIONALISM

How effective have you been in the past hour? What have you completed?

SMARTIN-UP™ YOUR PROFESSIONALISM

If a client got into your car right now what kind of impression would they get?

SMARTIN-UP™ YOUR PROFESSIONALISM

If someone asks an inappropriate question, simply say: "That is personal subject, may we talk about something else."

SMARTIN-UP™ YOUR PROFESSIONALISM

If we compromise our values we cease to be who we are.

SMARTIN-UP™ YOUR PROFESSIONALISM

If you drive slow, please stay in the right hand lane. There is a reason that person is in a hurry.

SMARTIN-UP™ YOUR PROFESSIONALISM

If you must no longer due business with a client, discuss this with them in person. Never by email or mail.

SMARTIN-UP™ YOUR PROFESSIONALISM

If you tell someone you only have 5 minutes to talk, when the 5 minutes is up tell them you need to go.

SMARTIN-UP™ YOUR PROFESSIONALISM

Professionals use the words "I apologize" in lieu of "I am sorry." The latter has a negative connotation.

SMARTIN-UP™ YOUR PROFESSIONALISM

In communicating, the receiver is most important not the sender. What you hear is more important than what I say.

SMARTIN-UP™ YOUR PROFESSIONALISM

It is best to arrive no more than 10 minutes early for an appointment. More than 10 is an inconvenience.

SMARTIN-UP™ YOUR PROFESSIONALISM

Just a reminder that it is rude to walk around with a blue tooth in your ear. When not talking, remove it.

SMARTIN-UP™ YOUR PROFESSIONALISM

Leaders are self-aware, They can observe their actions and the conduct of others in a "non-reactive" manner.

SMARTIN-UP™ YOUR PROFESSIONALISM

Look at your fingernails. What do they say about you? Clean, neat, professional... People notice!

SMARTIN-UP™ YOUR PROFESSIONALISM

A high level of energy is one of the best predictors of an entrepreneur's success.

SMARTIN-UP™ YOUR PROFESSIONALISM

Men are judged by their watch and their shoes, women by their purse and shoes. All of us by our cell phone model.

SMARTIN-UP™ YOUR PROFESSIONALISM

Never underestimate the value of enthusiasm. Get excited about what you do to help your customers!

SMARTIN-UP™ YOUR PROFESSIONALISM

On Sunday, try not to call anyone on the phone before 12:00 noon. It is the polite thing to do.

SMARTIN-UP™ YOUR PROFESSIONALISM

Only cut one or two pieces of meat at a time. We only cut all the meat for children.

SMARTIN-UP™ YOUR PROFESSIONALISM

Please do not lick your fingers while you are eating in public.

SMARTIN-UP™ YOUR PROFESSIONALISM

Please hold the door open for the person behind you. Look them in the eye and smile.

SMARTIN-UP™ YOUR PROFESSIONALISM

Professional women should not paint their nails blue, black, etc. if they want to be taken seriously.

SMARTIN-UP™ YOUR PROFESSIONALISM

Professionals arrive to work and to appts 10 minutes early. What time did you start work this morning?

SMARTIN-UP™ YOUR PROFESSIONALISM

Professionals have a commanding presence and strike a commanding stance.

SMARTIN-UP™ YOUR PROFESSIONALISM

Professionals know that it is more important to be respected than to be liked. Be accountable!

SMARTIN-UP™ YOUR PROFESSIONALISM

Professionals open their email with a greeting and end their email with a proper closing.

SMARTIN-UP™ YOUR PROFESSIONALISM

Try not to use your body language to end a conversation (tapping your foot, checking your watch, looking around).

SMARTIN-UP™ YOUR PROFESSIONALISM

Reflect on the lessons of the past in order to make sound decisions today and for the future.

SMARTIN-UP™ YOUR PROFESSIONALISM

Refrain from interrupting and correcting someone while they are speaking. Let them finish their thought.

SMARTIN-UP™ YOUR PROFESSIONALISM

Remember to be aware of your voice volume and adapt it to your surroundings.

SMARTIN-UP™ YOUR PROFESSIONALISM

Remember to polish/clean your shoes, belt, computer bag and/or purse on a regular basis. Look polished!

SMARTIN-UP™ YOUR PROFESSIONALISM

Sales knowledge is only one quarter of the presentation. Body language, tone of voice and professionalism get the sale!

SMARTIN-UP™ YOUR PROFESSIONALISM

Show how successful you are by sharing your knowledge with others.

SMARTIN-UP™ YOUR PROFESSIONALISM

Sometimes we don't realize we are emitting negative energy in our words. It can keep you from employment.

SMARTIN-UP™ YOUR PROFESSIONALISM

Successful people often ask themselves, "What am I willing to do to become even better at what I do?"

SMARTIN-UP™ YOUR PROFESSIONALISM

Take time to connect with a family member or friend that you have not contacted in a while.

SMARTIN-UP™ YOUR PROFESSIONALISM

The foundation for your brand is your reputation, be a good person that cares about and helps others.

SMARTIN-UP™ YOUR PROFESSIONALISM

The weekend is a good time for extra grooming. Look at your fingernails, cuticles and toe nails.

SMARTIN-UP™ YOUR PROFESSIONALISM

Treat all people with kindness and courtesy. See the soul, not the vessel. We are all so very special.

SMARTIN-UP™ YOUR PROFESSIONALISM

Try not to put your chin in your open palm while listening to someone. Looks like you are bored and can be perceived as rude.

SMARTIN-UP™ YOUR PROFESSIONALISM

Turn away from people when about to cough or sneeze.

SMARTIN-UP™ YOUR PROFESSIONALISM

Was your last email a novella? Messages should be concise, polite and to the point.

SMARTIN-UP™ YOUR PROFESSIONALISM

We show respect for someone by not interrupting them while they are speaking. Listen, then ask a question.

SMARTIN-UP™ YOUR PROFESSIONALISM

What type of pen do you carry with you? A lime green plastic one or a nice business style pen?

SMARTIN-UP™ YOUR PROFESSIONALISM

When communicating try not to use the words never, always or sometimes. Be specific.

SMARTIN-UP™ YOUR PROFESSIONALISM

When getting feedback, listen without interrupting, justifying or explaining.

SMARTIN-UP™ YOUR PROFESSIONALISM

When introducing someone, the first person's name you say is always the higher ranking person.

SMARTIN-UP™ YOUR PROFESSIONALISM

When networking remember the 80/20 rule. Listen 80% of the time and talk 20% of the time.

SMARTIN-UP™ YOUR PROFESSIONALISM

When sending a thank you note remember this acronym: G.E.T.

G – Mention the gift they gave you.

E – Express how it made you feel.

T – Thank them.

SMARTIN-UP™ YOUR PROFESSIONALISM

When taking candy to clients, be sure to have some sugar free candy as well. Many people are diabetic.

SMARTIN-UP™ YOUR PROFESSIONALISM

When was the last time you polished your belt? Shoes and belts must be kept clean and polished.

SMARTIN-UP™ YOUR PROFESSIONALISM

When you are in someone's office, do not sit down until you have been asked.

SMARTIN-UP™ YOUR PROFESSIONALISM

When you enter a room, refrain from loudly greeting someone who is across the room.

SMARTIN-UP™ YOUR PROFESSIONALISM

When you see someone struggling to put their coat on, help them by holding the coat by the collar.

SMARTIN-UP™ YOUR PROFESSIONALISM

Who have you taken for granted lately? Tell them how much you appreciate the little things they do !

SMARTIN-UP™ YOUR PROFESSIONALISM

Work-Life balance is imperative for good health, both mentally and physically.

SMARTIN-UP™ YOUR PROFESSIONALISM

You do not have to raise your voice when talking to someone from a different country. They hear you.

SMARTIN-UP™ YOUR PROFESSIONALISM

You should not sit down in someone's office without asking permission first.

SMARTIN-UP™ YOUR PROFESSIONALISM

When joining in on a conversation, remember to match your mood to the mood of the group.

SMARTIN-UP™ YOUR PROFESSIONALISM

In America, stand 2 feet from the person to whom you are speaking. Any closer is invading their space.

SMARTIN-UP™ YOUR PROFESSIONALISM

A hat should not be worn while you are dining at a table. It is considered disrespectful.

SMARTIN-UP™ YOUR PROFESSIONALISM

A slower smile is more sincere. We know a genuine smile by the look in your eye and rise of your cheeks.

SMARTIN-UP™ YOUR PROFESSIONALISM

Wear a conversation starter on your lapel. An organization pin or a pin that represents your interests.

SMARTIN-UP™ YOUR PROFESSIONALISM

Are you respectful? Are your children?
Manners (etiquette) help increase respect!

SMARTIN-UP™ YOUR PROFESSIONALISM

As with politics and religion, be careful discussing weight. There may be a health reason for a weight loss.

SMARTIN-UP™ YOUR PROFESSIONALISM

At a business meal, sit at right angles to your guest. Try to avoid sitting between two guests.

SMARTIN-UP™ YOUR PROFESSIONALISM

Avoid words and actions that put other people down. It reflects more on you than on them.

SMARTIN-UP™ YOUR PROFESSIONALISM

When networking/
visiting, refrain from
giving unsolicited
advice!

SMARTIN-UP™ YOUR PROFESSIONALISM

Be kind and treat people with respect. That applies to everyone you encounter during the course of your day!

SMARTIN-UP™ YOUR PROFESSIONALISM

Be prepared to leave a message if the person you have called does not answer the phone. Try not to use "ums" or "uhs" in your message.

SMARTIN-UP™ YOUR PROFESSIONALISM

Be the first to open and hold the door for the person in front of you or behind you.

SMARTIN-UP™ YOUR PROFESSIONALISM

Before walking into someone's office or cubicle, call or email to see if they have a minute to speak.

SMARTIN-UP™ YOUR PROFESSIONALISM

Business casual gotten too casual at your office? Many are rolling out new dress codes for Fall.

SMARTIN-UP™ YOUR PROFESSIONALISM

Challenge the status quo, dress business professional. People will see that you exude success.

SMARTIN-UP™ YOUR PROFESSIONALISM

Determine how long you want a phone call to last, and then time it with a stopwatch. Use your time wisely.

SMARTIN-UP™ YOUR PROFESSIONALISM

Do not put your napkin in your lap until the host/hostess does so first.

SMARTIN-UP™ YOUR PROFESSIONALISM

Do you know the proper way to get in and out of a car? Yes, there is a proper way.

SMARTIN-UP™ YOUR PROFESSIONALISM

Do you use your power to put people in their place or to help others rise to their potential?

SMARTIN-UP™ YOUR PROFESSIONALISM

Refrain from backbiting. What you say always comes back to bite you.

SMARTIN-UP™ YOUR PROFESSIONALISM

Do not pretend you aren't complaining when you are. You increase the chance of annoying your listeners.

SMARTIN-UP™ YOUR PROFESSIONALISM

Email should be replied to within at least 24 hours, and preferably within the same working day.

SMARTIN-UP™ YOUR PROFESSIONALISM

Excessive lowering of the voice often occurs in men who are insecure about themselves.

SMARTIN-UP™ YOUR PROFESSIONALISM

Focus on solutions, not problems. People prefer to be around problem solvers, not whiners.

SMARTIN-UP™ YOUR PROFESSIONALISM

Good posture produces a feeling of self-control, self-confidence and indicates alertness.

SMARTIN-UP™ YOUR PROFESSIONALISM

Hold internal classes for your employees on how to manage their personal finances in today's world.

SMARTIN-UP™ YOUR PROFESSIONALISM

It is best not to use email to discuss confidential information.

SMARTIN-UP™ YOUR PROFESSIONALISM

If a person is comfortable, it is reflected in their hands. Be observant of others and yourself.

SMARTIN-UP™ YOUR PROFESSIONALISM

If someone does not return your call right away, it's not you. They are just busy. Try to be patient and tolerant.

SMARTIN-UP™ YOUR PROFESSIONALISM

When was the last time you updated your business card? Do you look "outdated" on paper?

SMARTIN-UP™ YOUR PROFESSIONALISM

Five frequently misspelled words: calendar, cemetery, conscience, conscious and conscientious.

SMARTIN-UP™ YOUR PROFESSIONALISM

When someone helps with your bags, tip them $2/small-medium bags & $5 for larger/heavy bags/golf clubs/huge boxes.

SMARTIN-UP™ YOUR PROFESSIONALISM

Networking works both ways, if you want them to help you, you should be just as willing to help them.

SMARTIN-UP™ YOUR PROFESSIONALISM

Keep your word. If you say you will do something, do it.

ABOUT THE AUTHOR

Sindy is an international speaker, author and coach. Her company Smartin International provides seminars, workshops, keynotes and breakout sessions on Business Professionalism, American and International Protocol, Presentation Skills, and Business and Personal Etiquette.

Sindy has provided programs and coaching to Fortune 500 companies, universities, and national conferences, in addition to appearing as a featured guest on radio and television programs. She is an author of various articles for newspapers, magazines, on-line publications and the book "Are You a Duck, an Elephant or a Mouse? How are you perceived when you walk into a room?"

She is married to Bob Martin and has two children, two dogs and two cats. They live in High Point, North Carolina, USA.

Sindy Martin posts a Smartin-Up Your Professionalism tweet everyday on twitter.

Follow her at www.twitter.com/sindymartin